Gus

Jolanda Haverkamp & Anita de Vries

Written by
Jolanda Haverkamp

Illustrated by:
Anita de Vries

Translated from Dutch by:
Susanne Chumbley and Kelly Ljubojev

Published by:
Graviant educatieve uitgaven, Doetinchem

© June 2016

ISBN 978-9491337741

Although this book is compiled with care, neither the authors nor the publisher accept any liability for the fact that the use of what is offered does not meet the needs or expectations of the end user, nor for any errors or omissions.

Foreword

This beautifully and colourful illustrated book is very
suitable for children and people around them who are confronted
with gender dysphoria.

When you have a very good idea about who you are, but your surroundings
expect different behaviour from you because of your appearance; that can be
confusing. Who are you then? Your inside or your outside?

If only we could see

what your heart shows

then everything

would be beautiful

like you

Not to be

what is expected

but acting

to make the world

smile at you

(translated from a poem

by Mark Kronenburcht

3

Far, very far from here is an extraordinary land.
It is the land of the Key geese.
It is a peaceful place where nothing ever changes.
Blue is blue.
Orange is orange.
It always has been.

In the big bubble house
the little unborn goslings calmly slide down
through the tubes.

They softly slide further and further.

To eventually become who they are.

Blue goslings through the blue tubes.

Orange goslings through the orange tubes.

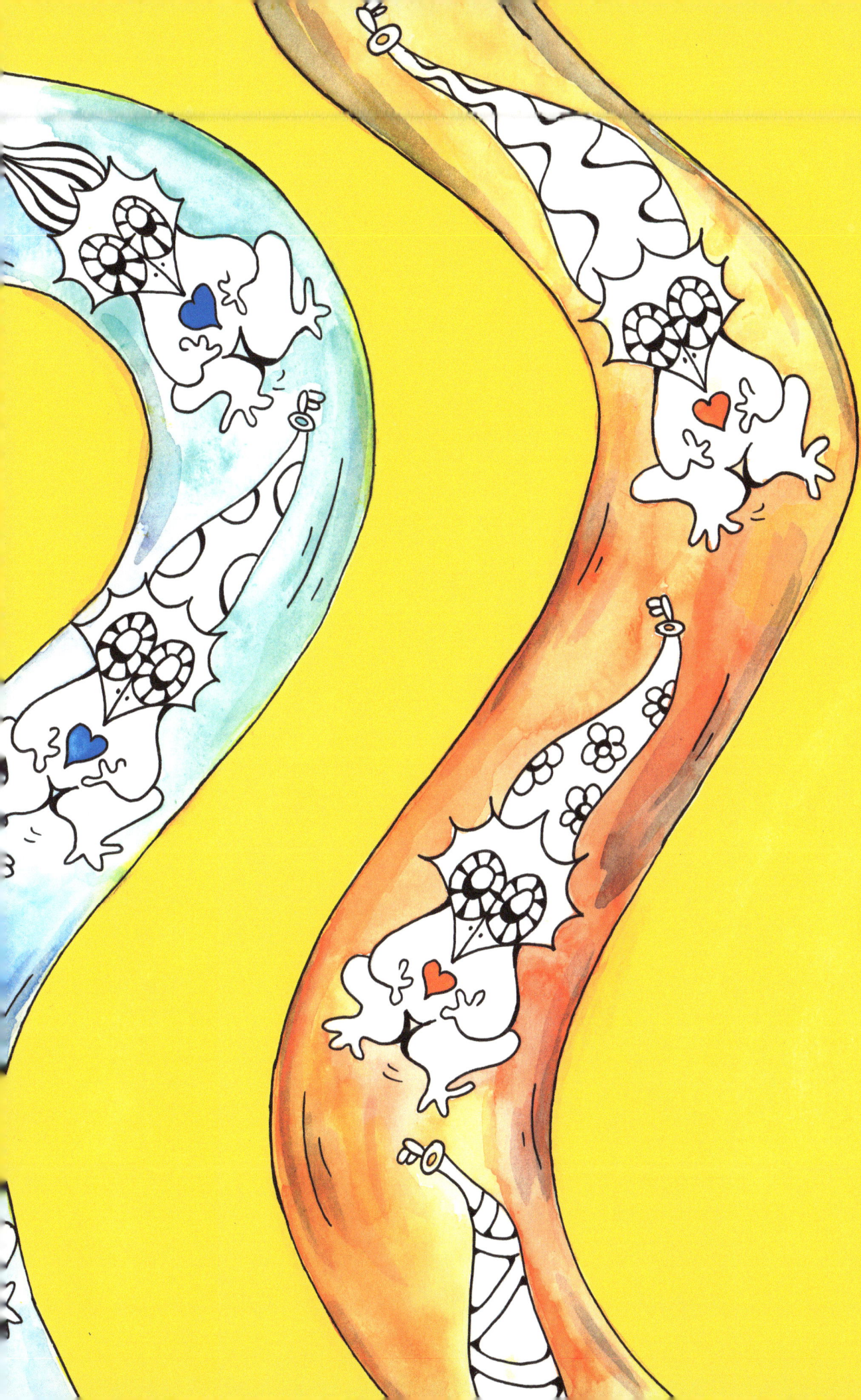

A blue Key gosling
is always blue.

An orange gosling
is always orange.

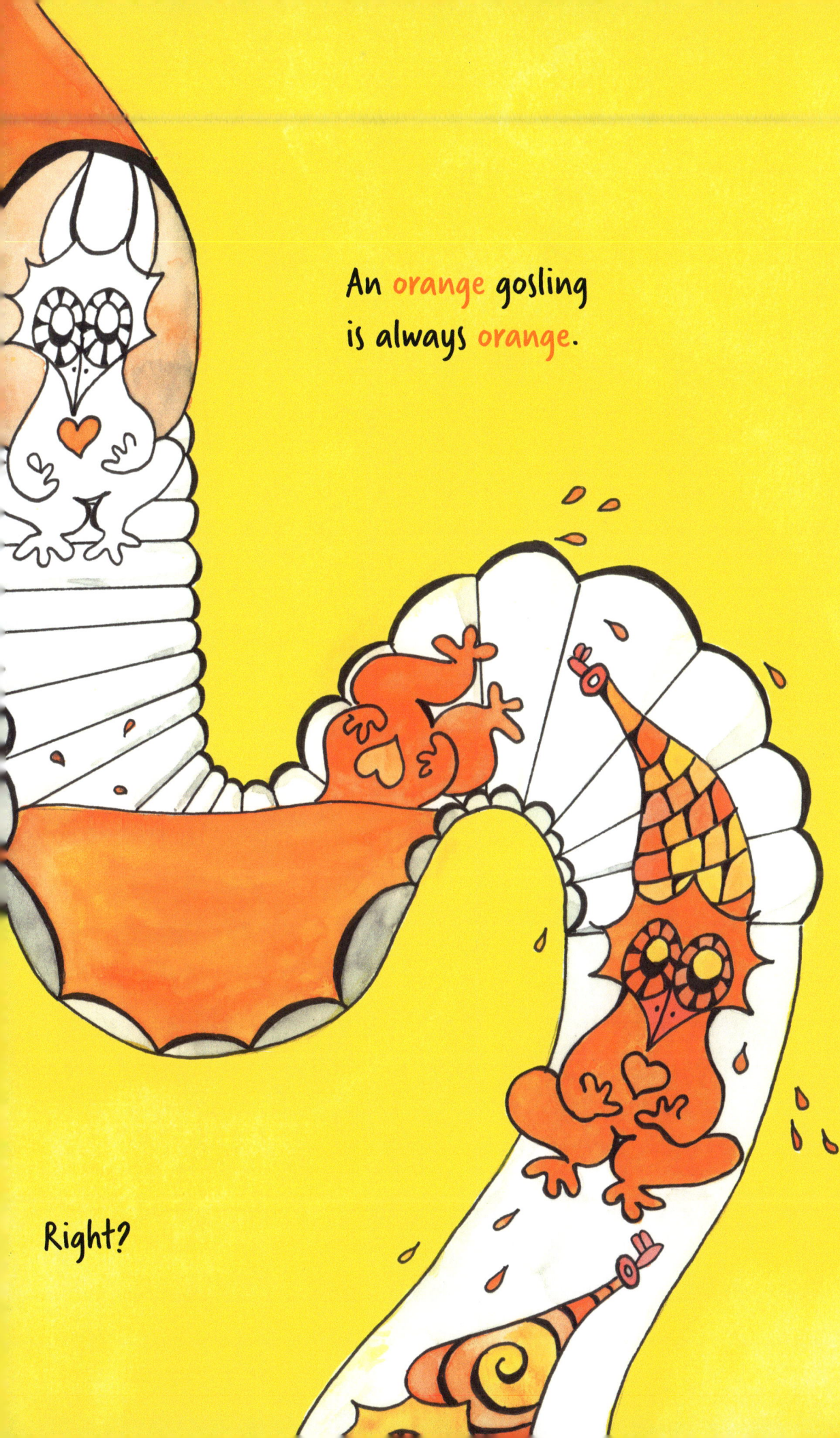

Right?

Gus
the gosling with
the blue heart

moves to the left,
turns right,
and accidentally rolls into the orange bath.

A day like any other.

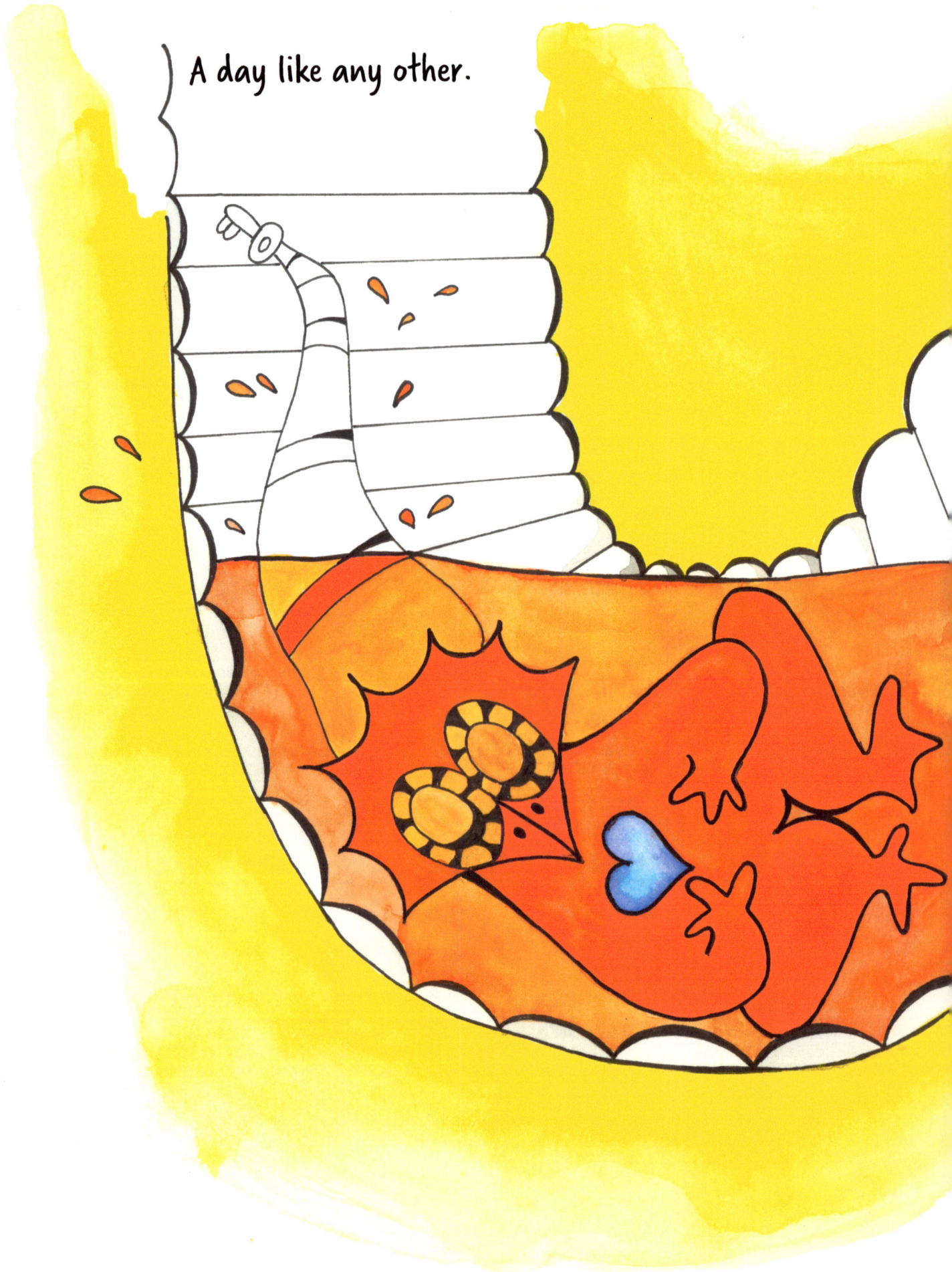

Gus, with the blue heart, also slides further through the warm, light, orange tube.

on his way to becoming who he is.

Blue.
Orange.

or blue?
or maybe orange?

A peaceful place.

The blue goslings
always do
blue things
together.

Happily.

The orange goslings do things
always on their own.

Blissfully.

Gus's blue little heart beats warm,
deep inside his orange body.

Gus and Pom are old enough. They look in the mirror at each other and at their blue friends.

Their hearts close and little hatches with a keyhole appear.
They can only use their keys when they are grown up.

Play!

Gus has a little purple ball.
Pom the big green one.

Gus throws.
But Pom doesn't throw it back.

Pom doesn't want to play together.
Pom is orange, she wants to play on her own.

Jock surely wants
to play together
with the rope!

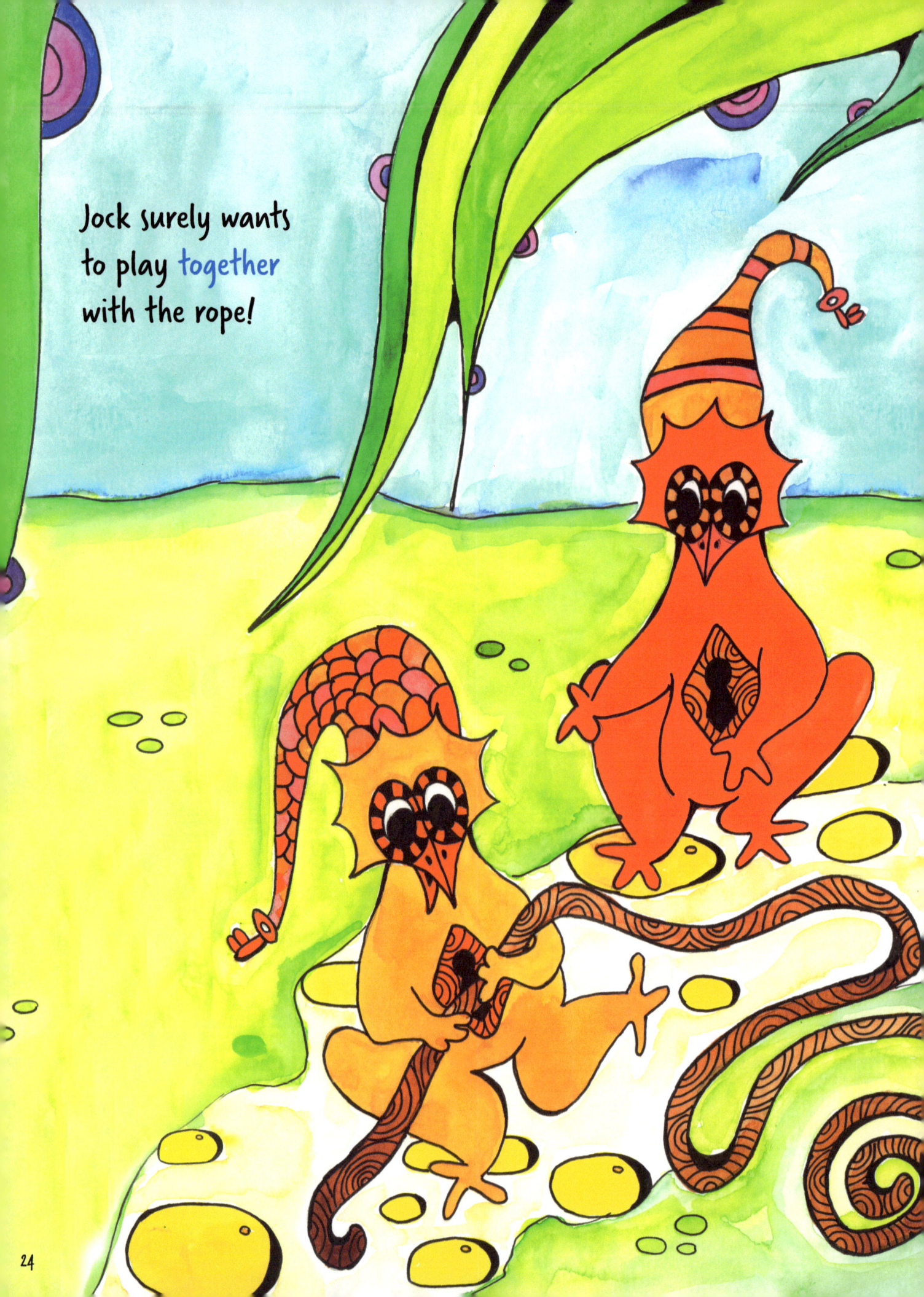

But Jock doesn't want
to play together.
He is orange, he wants
to play on his own.

Gus runs after Fifi.
But Fifi also doesn't want to play together.

Fifi is orange, she wants to
play on her own.

They all want

to play on their OWN.

27

Gus looks around feeling sad.
What now?

The orange goslings play alone.
All of them.
Always.

Gus really wants to play together.
So desperately.

Gus watches the blue goslings.
They play together.

All of them.
Always.

Gus shyly
approaches them.

Everybody looks up.
Surprised.

Gus is orange.
Not blue.

Pom runs after Gus.
"You are orange Gus!"

Gus stops.

"I don't want to play on my own."
"But we are orange!", says Pom.

"You are orange
and want to do
everything on
your own.

I am....
I want to play together!"
And Gus carries
on walking.

Music sounds.
It is beautiful.
Gus stands still.

He sees blue Key goslings
playing music together.

His heart feels warm and beats faster than normal.

He lays his hand on his heart
and feels the warmth
of his mysterious,
but familiar hatch.

With his other hand, he grabs
the little key on his hat.

Gus follows the sweet tunes of the music
and walks towards a group of blue
Key goslings.

They stop playing music and look
surprised at the orange gosling in their midst.

Gus moves along with them
to the music and feels
his warm heart, beating
behind the familiar hatch.

They look puzzled at Gus.

"What are you doing Gus?
We are blue!
You don't belong here!

You better
go back."

A tear rolls down Gus's cheek.

His heart feels freezing cold when
he lays his hand on the little hatch.

The next day all
the little Key goslings
go to school for
the first time.

KIND

STRONG

BLUE

FA

"What would you like to be when you grow up?", asks the teacher.
"Happy?"   "Strong?"   "Kind?"   "Pretty?"

"Blue", whispers Gus.

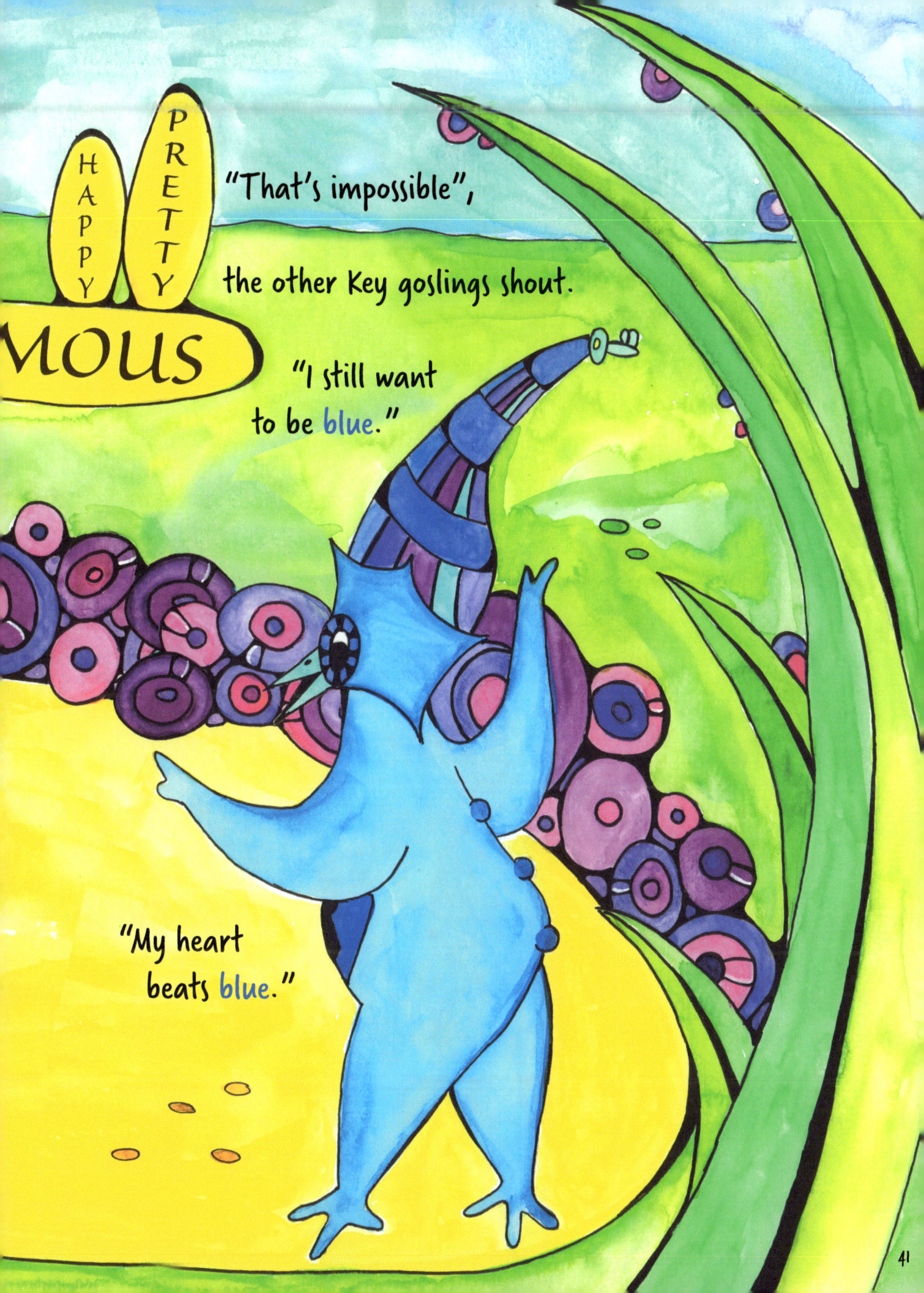

Finally, the day arrives that Gus and Pom are old enough to open their little hatches and to look inside their heart to discover who they really are.

Pom opens her hatch.
Gus sees a warm
orange glow
coming out.

Kind it says in big letters.

Gus takes his own little key
and carefully unlocks his hatch.

He barely dares to look.

Brave

And beautiful beams of
blue light are shinning
from his heart.

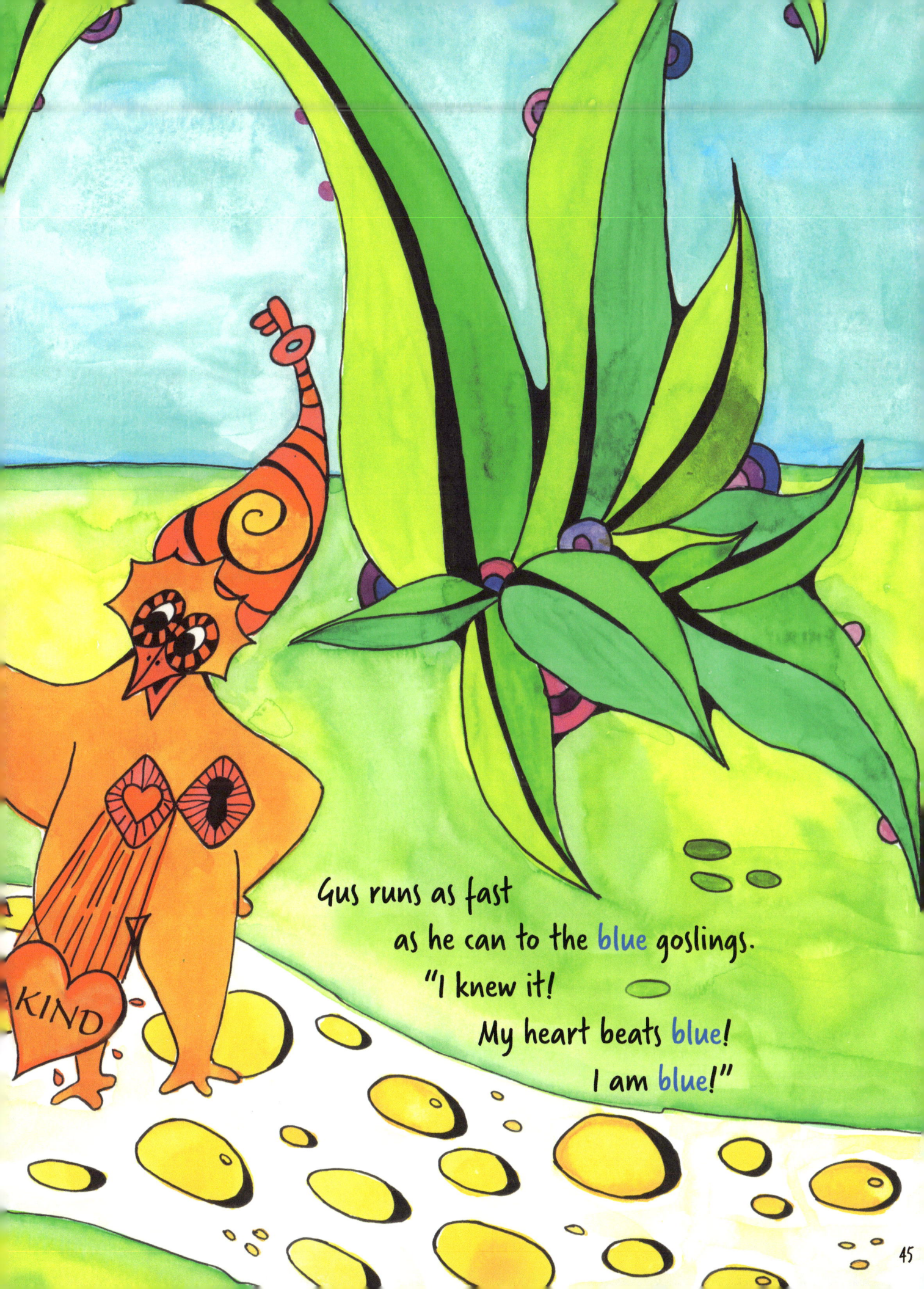

Gus runs as fast
as he can to the blue goslings.
"I knew it!
My heart beats blue!
I am blue!"

Pom looks at Gus
and says happily:

BRAVE

KIND

BRAVE

BRAVE

"You are not the colour
of your outside,

but you are

the colour of your

heart."

And from that day on, Gus is known as the little orange gosling that does blue things.

And also as the little orange gosling
with the big, brave,

blue

heart

This book can help to give insight and meaning to children who are confronted with gender dysphoria.

It is clear from the start of this book that Gus is blue and, therefore, displays blue behaviour. The fact that his outside appearance is orange forces people around him to expect orange behaviour of him. This is difficult for Gus. Children, but also adults, can imagine that Gus wants to do blue things because he 'is' blue.

And that he finds it hard to be like orange geese, even though he looks like them. What happens to Gus will be very recognisable. Everybody can easily place themselves in his position and wonder how to deal with it.

And in the end, this applies to us all.

We don't have keys to our hearts, we have to rely on what others say, they feel and believe about themselves. It is important not to judge children who have to walk this path.

Trust who they are, regardless of their appearance.

Be your own kind of beautiful!